Are You Ready for Spring?

Sheila Anderson

Lerner Publications Company
Minneapolis

To Aidan
Chiaokhiao

Lerner Publications Company
A division of Lerner Publishing Group, Inc.
241 First Avenue North
Minneapolis, MN 55401 U.S.A.

Website address: www.lernerbooks.com

Library of Congress Cataloging-in-Publication Data

Anderson, Sheila.
    Are You Ready for Spring? / by Sheila M. Anderson.
        p.   cm. — (Lightning bolt books™ – Our four seasons)
    Includes index.
    ISBN 978-0-7613-4584-8 (lib. bdg. : alk. paper)
    1. Spring—Juvenile literature. I. Title.
    QB637.5.A53 2010
    508.2—dc22   2009016409

Manufactured in the United States of America
1 – BP – 12/15/09

Contents

Sights and Sounds of Spring

Sploosh! *Sploosh!* Do you hear that? It is the sound of rubber boots splashing in deep, muddy puddles!

It is spring.
The snow has melted, leaving splooshy, squishy mud in its place.

Two boys play in mud puddles.

5

Listen! You can hear birds' wings flapping as they fly to and fro. They work in pairs to build their nests.

A bird lines its nest with soft fluff.

Spring Weather

Heavy, gray clouds move in. It looks as if it might rain. Don't forget to bring your umbrella!

Raindrops the size of pennies begin to fall. *Plop, plop, plop.*

Rain taps against the windows in a springtime shower.

Rain makes a *patter, patter, patter* sound on rooftops, sidewalks, and umbrellas.

9

Thunder rumbles in the distance.

Lightning flashes in
bright zigzags
across the sky

Springing to Life

Flowers and trees need spring rains to grow. Tiny shoots emerge from the dark, moist earth.

New leaves poke out of a melting snowbank.

Knotty buds form on trees.
They will become delicate,
bright green leaves.

Spring brings lots of activity. Birds lay eggs. Soon we will hear the *peep, peep, peep* of newly hatched chicks.

Hungry baby birds call out to their parents.

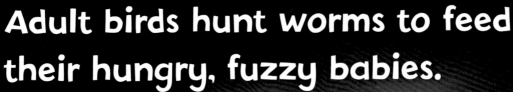

Adult birds hunt worms to feed
their hungry, fuzzy babies.

In springtime, mother deer give birth to fawns. These babies' coats are sprinkled with white dots.

The white dots on a fawn's coat help it hide in the grass.

Bears begin to emerge from their cozy winter dens. They are hungry after long months of hibernation.

A grizzly bear comes out of its den. The bear slept in the den all winter.

Everyone feels energized by the change in the weather.

The Spring World

As the weather gets warmer, families play together outdoors.

This family is taking a hike.

Colorful kites *whoosh* through the sky, whisked along on brisk breezes.

19

People dig in the earth to plant seeds in flower beds and gardens. Soon plants will grow from the seeds.

Flowers begin to bloom, coloring the world with bright pinks, yellows, and reds.

Flowers poke through last year's dead leaves.

Insects flit here and there. Bees buzz from flower to flower.

Animals begin to shed their winter coats.

This bison is shedding its heavy winter coat.

Summer Is Coming

The temperature gets warmer and warmer. It is time to pack away our bulky winter clothes!

Days get longer and longer.

Long days mean more time to play!

Puddles and mud begin to dry up. Days are bright and warm.

Summer is on its way.

What will you do in the summer?

How Do Chicks Hatch?

Many baby animals are born in the spring. One of them is the baby chicken, or chick.

Mother chickens lay eggs when they are ready to have chicks. One tiny chick is inside each egg. The mother chicken sits on the eggs after she lays them. Soon the chicks are ready to hatch.

A chick picks at its eggshell when it's ready to hatch. This is called pipping. A chick has a tiny "horn" on the top of its beak. The horn is called an egg tooth. The chick uses its egg tooth to break out of its egg.

It's a lot of work for a chick to break out of its egg! The chick is wet and tired when it first breaks free. It may lie still and rest for a few hours. Soon its downy feathers have dried. The chick is ready to explore its surroundings.

A chick's egg tooth falls off within a day after the chick hatches. The chick starts growing feathers just a few weeks later. She'll look more like a chicken than a chick in no time!

A chick watches another chick hatch.

Glossary

breeze: a mild wind

bud: a leaf or flower that has not yet opened

emerge: to come out

energize: to become active and full of energy

fawn: a baby deer

hatch: to break out from inside an egg

hibernation: the practice of spending winter in a sleeplike state

moist: wet

shed: to lose fur

Further Reading

Baxter, Nicola. *Spring*. Mankato, MN: Sea-to-Sea Publications, 2009.

Enchanted Learning: Earth's Seasons http://www.enchantedlearning.com/subjects/astronomy/planets/earth/seasons.shtml

Glaser, Linda. *It's Spring!* Minneapolis: Millbrook Press, 2002.

Pfeffer, Wendy. *A New Beginning: Celebrating the Spring Equinox*. New York: Dutton Children's Books, 2008.

Ray, Mary Lyn. *Mud*. San Diego: Harcourt, 2001.

Schnur, Steven. *Spring Thaw*. New York: Viking, 2000.

Watch a Chick Hatch http://www.msichicago.org/online-science/videos/video-detail/activities/the-hatchery

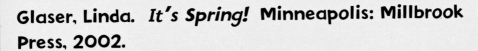

Index

Photo Acknowledgments

The images in this book are used with the permission of: © Gerry Lemmo, pp. 1, 6, 10, 11, 15, 21, 27; © Almir1968/Dreamstime.com, p. 2; © Mike Ford/SuperStock, p. 4; © age fotostock/SuperStock, pp. 5, 9, 20, 23, 29; © Steve Satushek/Photographer's Choice/Getty Images, p. 7; © Stockbyte/Getty Images, p. 8; © Photononstop/SuperStock, pp. 12, 13; © Flirt/SuperStock, p. 14; © Shane Moore/Animals Animals, p. 16; © Westend61/SuperStock, p. 17; © Kwame Zikomo/SuperStock, p. 18; © Pacific Stock/SuperStock, p. 19; © Karlene Schwartz, p. 22; © Hemis.fr/SuperStock, p. 24; © Ed Simpson/Photographer's Choice/Getty Images, p. 25; © Prisma/SuperStock, p. 26; © Le Do/Dreamstime.com, p. 30; © Erkki Makkonen/Dreamstime.com, p. 31 (both).

Front cover: © Darrell Gulin/Photographer's Choice/Getty Images (top); © Chris Stein/Stone/Getty Images (bottom)